*To Karen
my dearest daughter
Without her I would
have lost all my dreams
Love,
Mother*

The Poet's Domain

Collections of Poems
by Writers in Delaware, Maryland, Virginia
and the District of Columbia

Volume Seven
Footprints on the Sands of Time

Compiled and Edited by
Joseph D. Adams

"Books Worth Your Time"
Box 431 • Painter, Virginia 23420

Copyright © 1993 by ROAD Publishers

All rights reserved
including the right of reproduction
in whole or in part in any form.

Published by
ROAD Publishers
33412 Lankford Highway
Painter, Va. 23420

Designed by Donna L. Robinson

ISBN 1-880016-11-7 **6.95**

Printed in the United States of America

CONTENTS

A Note from the Publisher   xi
The Editor's Preface   xv

BARBARA H. ACHILLES, *Vienna, VA*
Hillary's Headband   1

PATRICIA S. ADLER, *Woodbridge, VA*
Through a Lens   2

LOLETE FALCK BARLOW, *Camp Springs, MD*
Choices   3
Elegy   3

MARY KAY BELTER, *Vienna, VA*
Reactions   4

PATSY ANNE BICKERSTAFF, *Weyers Cave, VA*
Maggie Walker in the Van Lew Garden   5

SHEILA CARDANO, *Cape Charles, VA*
Old Age   6

ROBERT ALLEN CARTER, *Richmond, VA*
Observations on the Beach   7

ANTONIA CHAMBERS, *Fenwick Island, DE*
Pietá   8

SUSAN D. CLARK, *Nokesville, VA*
Modern Medicine   9

RHEA L. COHEN, *Greenbelt, MD*
Footprints   10

ELINOR CUBBAGE, *Hebron, MD*
On the Surface   11

SALLY DUNNING, *Woodbridge, VA*
    Humble Perspectives   12

NEAL MICHAEL DWYER, *Waldorf, MD*
    Un Commencement   13

MARGARET EDWARDS, *Earlysville, VA*
    Reflections   14
    Tread Lightly   14

LADDIE FISHER, *Roanoke, VA*
    Hand and Glove   15

LINDA BETH FRISTOE, *Front Royal, VA*
    The Prince Who Loved Me Darkly   16
    Lotus Flower   17

GERTRUDE GUNTHER, *Onancock, VA*
    Music   18
    The Polite Parlor   18

JOANN HARTMAN, *Waterford, VA*
    The Golden Gate   19

BARBARA McKAY HEWIN, *Williamsburg, VA*
    Nightmare Alice   20

JANE H. HU, *Potomac, MD*
    Tea House   21

NANCY STUART HUNDLEY, *Boydton, VA*
    The Way Home   22

ROSALIE S. JENNINGS, *Edinburg, VA*
    The Mayor's Shield   23

AVAH JOHNSON, *McLean, VA*
    Epicedium   24

AGNES NASMITH JOHNSTON, *Alexandria, VA*
    Appalachian Trails   25
    Cincinnati Girl   25
    Flyers   26

JEAN P. KLOTZBACH, *Columbia, MD*
My Mother Said   27
You Are Old   27
Memory   28

MARY ROSE KNAPP, *Dale City, VA*
Consumed   29

OLIVE S. LANHAM, *Daytona Beach, FL*
Dance on the Dunes   30
Destination   30

MARY ANTIL LEDERMAN, *Charlottesville, VA*
Footprints of the Soul   31
Sunny Side Out   32

JOAN LEOTTA, *Burke, VA*
Grand Canyon Visit   33

JOSEPH LEWIS, *Williamsburg, VA*
Starry Night   34

HARRIET CAMPBELL LITTLE, *Beaverdam, VA*
The Silent Seconds   35

KATIE GOLDSTEIN LORBER, *Columbia, MD*
South Florida I   36
South Florida II   36

MICHAEL HUGH LYTHGOE, *Gainesville, VA*
Aubade for Archaeology   37
A Winter Cure   38

JOAN MALOOF, *Quantico, MD*
The Sound that Water Makes As It Pours Through the Alphabet of Names   39
Cycles   40

ALICE SHOGER MAWDSLEY, *Lynchburg, VA*
One Way   41
I Shall Weep For You   41

JAMES L. MAWDSLEY, *Lynchburg, VA*
To a Friend   42

JONATHAN R. MAWDSLEY, *Lynchburg, VA*
To the author of the article "What   43
the world will be like in the year 1984"

DOROTHY W. MILLNER, *Alexandria, VA*
On the Stairs   44

ROBERT R. MONTGOMERY, *Hartfield, VA*
Diogenes   45
Lost Toddler   45

DAVID J. PARTIE, *Lynchburg, VA*
Looking at a Photograph of Stephen Crane, 1894   46

PATRICIA ROYAL PERKINSON, *Topping, VA*
50th Reunion   47

TAD PHIPPS, *Blacksburg, VA*
Color Blind   48

RICHARD RAYMOND, III, *Midlothian, VA*
Beach Rover   49
Seasons   50

FRED F. RICHARDSON, *Machipongo, VA*
My Uncle's Shoes   51

EVELYN RITCHIE, *Richmond, VA*
Ordered Pair, Graphed ($x + y = 1$)   53
Ringing in My Ears   53
Waiting Up for My Son   54

LESLIE SANDS, *Smithfield, VA*
House for Sale   55

SANDRA GINN SCOVILLE, *Parksley, VA*
Flying   57

LYNDA SELF, *Norfolk, VA*
Sequel   58

SHIRLEY NESBIT SELLERS, *Norfolk, VA*
The Castle 59
Old Bay Line Steamer 59

HARRY B. SHEFTEL, *Washington, D.C.*
Bright Burning 60

ASKOLD SKALSKY, *Ijamsville, MD*
Metaphysic's End 61

BARBARA SMITH, *Newport News, VA*
Lady Liberty Weekend 62

WILLIAM REUBEN SMITH, *Lynchburg, VA*
Viewing the Great Nebula in the Dagger of Orion 63
Maturity 64

BRUCE SOUDERS, *Winchester, VA*
Ruminations in a Parking Lot 65
Apologia: A Collage of Remembrance 65

ISOBEL ROUTLY STEWART, *Woodbridge, VA*
The Dark Clouds Part 67
Appointment with the Vet 68

KATHRYN A. STRICKLAND, *Blacksburg, VA*
Hour Glass 69

HILDA (BOYCE) SWEIKHART, *Baltimore, MD*
A Humility of Valor 70
The Lamb's Cry 70

D. LYNN SYDOW, *Lebanon, VA*
Complements 71

CONSTANCE TUPPER, *Charlottesville, VA*
Dear Friend 73

GONNY VAN DEN BROEK, *Washington, D.C.*
For Him Who Thinks He Sinned 74
Before Boarding 74

EVELYN AMUEDO WADE, *Alexandria, VA*
Lists   76

TEMPLE WEST, *Norfolk, VA*
Mother Myth   77

CHARLOTTE WISE, *Nellysford, VA*
The Market of Words   78

MORAEG E. WOOD, *Charlottesville, VA*
Flotsam and Jetsam   79

ISRAEL ZOBERMAN, *Virginia Beach, VA*
Years Later   80
Places & Lovers   80

A Note from the Publisher

The Poet's Domain is ROAD Publishers' series of collected contemporary poetry by writers in or from Delaware, Maryland, Virginia, and the District of Columbia.

We proudly publish these special poetry collections in limited edition volumes. In addition to demonstrating that good poets are actively at work in the region, these books provide the quality showcase these fine poets deserve.

To keep poetry accessible to readers, ROAD Publishers offers these volumes at modest prices without sacrificing quality of production.

To date, the works of more than one hundred poets have appeared in the pages of *The Poet's Domain*. Future volumes will display greater numbers of quality works by greater numbers of fine regional poets. Key biographical information about the poets acquaints readers with the poets.

In the present volume, the poets address a number of concerns. They want to engage readers. Readers, in turn, may engage them through us.

Donna L. Robinson
Publisher

The best place to meet the poets of the region
is in
THE POET'S DOMAIN

Are there any ROAD Publishers books you want but cannot find in your bookstore? If so, order directly from us. You can get any ROAD Publishers book in print. Include the book's title, volume number, author, and ISBN number if you have it, along with a check or money order (do not send cash in the mails) for the full retail price plus $1.95 to cover shipping and handling. Virginia residents—please add 4.5 percent sales tax. Mail to:

ROAD Publishers, P.O. Box 431, Painter, VA 23420-0431.

The Editor's Preface

We take the title for the seventh volume of *The Poet's Domain* from "A Psalm of Life," by the great American teacher/poet Henry Wadsworth Longfellow (1807-1882). The poem first appeared in the September 1838 issue of the *Knickerbocker* magazine. In slightly altered form, the poem was included in *Voices of the Night* (Cambridge: 1839). Citations below are from the 1838 version.

Professor of modern languages at Bowdoin and later at Harvard, Longfellow introduced his students to an exceptional sweep of European literature. In addition to his classroom teaching, his anthology, *The Poets and Poetry of Europe*, brought European refinement into quite ordinary American households.

As a poet, Longfellow—the great teacher—domesticated European poetics and as a result his writings became a sort of cultural beacon, an illuminating and instructional force in American life. Always eminently quotable, he grew into America's most popular poet, perhaps the most beloved American poet of his time. The 20th-century consciousness, however, has not viewed his work with the same esteem his own generation bestowed upon it.

The reason may be that Longfellow's unquestioned convictions were intricately woven into the web of his writing. Many of those older unquestioned convictions have not survived the turbulent passage of years. In "A Psalm of Life," we find Harvard professor Longfellow, almost 32 years of age—in the guise of a young man pouring out his heart to the psalmist—not questioning life's significance or purpose, but confidently imparting to readers a series of imperative but occasionally inconsistent precepts. He declares with certitude the soul's immortality. Rejecting pleasure as life's aim and simultaneously disavowing this life as simply a vale of trial and tears, he maintains belief in progress. He declares actions that contribute to human progress to be life's heroic principle. Discarding the past and distrusting the future, he calls for struggle in the "glorious present."

To inspire us to action, he finally asserts:

> Lives of great men all remind us
>   We can make *our* lives sublime,
> And, departing, leave behind us
>   Footsteps on the sands of time.

> Footsteps, that, perhaps another,
> > Sailing o'er life's solemn main,
> A forlorn and shipwreck'd brother,
> > Seeing, shall take heart again.

We may forgive the chauvinism of his verses and of the period in which they were penned. But we have to question the way Longfellow figuratively portrayed the imprint of human *exempla*, particularly since it contradicts his earlier caution: "Let the dead Past bury its dead!" To motivate young men to "be up and doing," the young poet/teacher Longfellow offers as models the lives of great men. And after the young men have died (departed), they too—like the great men whom they had emulated—may leave "footprints on the sands of time," hardly a lasting legacy.

In an image that curiously summons up Robinson Crusoe's discovery of Friday's footprint on the beach, Longfellow further suggests that succeeding "forlorn and shipwreck'd" brothers' discovering footprints on the sands will give them reassurance. One takes solace, we suppose, in the knowledge that one does not struggle alone in life.

Now, fifteen and a half decades later, how do poets view the stamp of human activity? In the age of electronic tele-celebrity, with what certitude do poets regard human lives? On what scale do they weigh human values? The answers await us not in a twilight zone, but in the poet's domain.

> **Joseph D. Adams**
> *Fairfax, Virginia*
> February 1993

Barbara H. Achilles

Hillary's Headband

lies in the parking lot
as nervous rain
doodles overlapping circles
in puddles around
this down-turned crown.

Blue-red silk brushed
with blurred strokes of navy,
stretched taut across
a tortoise-shell spring
arched in a wide C,
abandoned on an iridescent oil slick.

Discarded in an epiphany
of political correctness.

Barbara H. Achilles (b. 1931, Knowlesville, NY), former music director, scriptwriter, and retired intelligence officer, graduated from the Eastman School of Music and the College of Arts and Sciences, University of Rochester. Her poetry has appeared in volumes 5 and 6 of *The Poet's Domain* and has been accepted for publication in *The Wall Street Journal*. She received prizes in Virginia and California state poetry society competitions. A member of the National League of American Pen Women, she resides in Vienna, VA, where she is currently working on a collection of profiles of minor historical figures.

Patricia S. Adler

Through a Lens

Patricia S. Adler
(b. 1938, Elizabeth, NJ),
French teacher for 20
years, is now studying
commercial art at
Northern Virginia
Community College.
This is her second
appearance in
The Poet's Domain.

I saw them
standing on the shore.
He faced the water
arms folded
close to his chest.
She faced him
hands on hips
head down,
serious.
She dropped her hands
outstretched,
as if to say,
"What more can I do?"
or
"Is that all you can say?"
Frustration.
He unfolded his arms
and reached toward her,
but she had turned
and didn't see
what I could
through a lens.

Lolete Falck Barlow

Lolete Falck Barlow
(b. 1932, Mobile, AL) divides her time between home in Camp Springs, MD, and "Bay View", a waterfront retreat in North Beach on the Chesapeake Bay. Past president of the Alexandria Branch, National League of American Pen Women, her award winning poems have appeared in numerous periodicals. She is currently Poetry Editor of the Pen Woman magazine.

Choices

I race through life at breakneck speed—
    No time to smell the roses.
I'm pieced and parceled where there's need,
    Or so my Id supposes.

That pace is mine; it's one I chose
    And so far, I've succeeded.
Although I long to be composed,
    I'd rather know I'm needed.

Elegy

My dear and loving father,
charming, witty, wise, and wonderful,
generous, intelligent, and kind,
creative, warm and unselfish,
sentimental, courtly, and fine
died
an alcoholic.

Mary K. Belter

Reactions

My misplaced reactions
laugh in my horror,
scream in consensual silence,
are jealous of another's joy,
bellow during consecration,
spill tears over beauty,
sneer at advice given,
ignore the needy,
shiver in the sun,
burrow into a light hearted hug,
cling during separation,
beg when strength is appropriate,
curse in the midst of prayer.

These awful movements from the core
never fit,
explode into overwhelming,
render me the fool.

All eyes stare curious loathing at me,
lost in my hysterics.
She looks away.
He clears his throat.
Eyes meet in common revulsion.
Others avert, change course
to avoid embarrassment.

I am exposed,
naked for all to see.

Mary K. Belter (b. 1948, Hobart, OK) studied biology at George Mason University and worked with the National Park Service for two years. Her work has appeared in several volumes of *The Poet's Domain*. She lives in Vienna, VA.

Patsy Anne Bickerstaff

Maggie Walker in the Van Lew Garden

Scrambling after a marmalade cat
in Crazy Bett's garden, Maggie Lena
disturbs a bough. Mockorange petals shower,
shine, cling in unraveling plaits,
collect in the lap of her pinafore,
fill her small dark hands. She laughs.
The blossoms are, this moment, silver coins
and she a princess. "Mama, look how rich!"
Rich indeed, with wealth
of freedom, won so hard; with hours
like treasure caskets, open, spilling over;
Rich with new gifts of ancient wisdom,
rich with youth, with dreams to build.
Slave's daughter, frolicking
in flowers, can she know
how tall are those tomorrows she will make?
how her brothers
will follow her through this new world
to dignity?
how little time she has
for childhood?

Patsy Anne Bickerstaff (b. 1940, Richmond, VA) appeared in volumes 1 and 6 of *The Poet's Domain*. Her work has been published in some 60 reviews and anthologies, and her book, *City Rain*, sold out in a limited edition. She lives in Weyers Cave, VA, and is recording secretary of the Poetry Society of Virginia. She is listed in *Writers in Virginia*, *Poets & Writers*, and the International *Who's Who of Poetry*.

Sheila Cardano

Old Age

How mysterious it is to grow old—
To live a fading day
To find the mind wandering
Drifting
                    slowly away.
Straining to see—
        unable to hear—
Watching a shaking hand,
        Faltering steps—
                stumbling—
Failing to understand.

Sheila Cardano (b. 1921, London, England) graduated from Royal Academy of Dramatic Art. She lived in Italy for over forty years before coming to rest on the Eastern Shore of Virginia. Her poems appeared in volumes 5 and 6 of *The Poet's Domain.*

Robert Allen Carter

Observations on the Beach

Robert Allen Carter (b. 1947, Baltimore, MD), is a historian and administrator with the Virginia Department of Historic Resources. A resident of Richmond, Virginia, he is the author of *Virginia Federalist in Dissent: A Life of Charles Fenton Mercer, 1778-1858*.

1

Beer bottle mosaic
Artless, prosaic.

2

A thousand shells.
Atrophied ears
Of old men
Who have heard
A thousand
Now-or-never tunes
On the dunes of the years.

3

Sand crabs scribble
While the paint is wet
On the useless taupe,
Then wash their hands
With sandy soap.
They are hirelings
To the last.
Who's your boss,
The patron of your art?
Eternal sea,
Iconoclast.

4

Like traps set along the shore,
Seaweed enshackles a deserted beach,
Writhing under the harrow.
Imagining nettles, the mind
Ponders human bondage,
Disputes weather.
The sea, knowing no sorrow,
Settles the argument.

5

At the edge of the sea
Upon a liquid looking glass,
She meets her beauty
Face to face.

She becomes
One of the clouds,
One of the seas.

Antonia Chambers

Pietá

Twenty-six years have passed since this I saw
Can marble speak of sorrow and of pain?
A chill goes through me and I stand in awe
That chiseled vein of stone is human vein.

Can marble speak of sorrow and of pain?
Can rock reveal the depth of heart?
That chiseled vein of stone is human vein
Is manifest in this great work of art.

Can rock reveal the depth of heart?
A mother's love, a mother's grief
Is manifest in this great work of art,
An expression of reverence and belief

A mother's love, a mother's grief,
Stone cold as death revealing death,
An expression of reverence and belief
Releasing to the world a dying breath.

Stone cold as death revealing death:
Michelangelo, what have you wrought?
Releasing to the world a dying breath
The Master to a master art has taught.

Michelangelo what have you wrought?
Death comes to life and gives to life new birth.
The Master to a master art has taught;
A piece of heaven has fallen to earth.

A chill goes through me and I stand in awe—
Twenty-six years have passed since this I saw.

Antonia Chambers (b. 1955, Niagara Falls, NY) is a writer and former government attorney (human rights and international law). She holds a B.A. in English from Niagara University (summa cum laude) and a J.D. from Notre Dame Law School. Her poetry has appeared in *Midwest Poetry Review* and several anthologies; her book of poems, *Sow the Wind*, will be published in 1993. A ten-year resident of Alexandria, VA, she currently lives in Fenwick Island, DE.

Susan D. Clark

Modern Medicine

Cubicles of gray and mauve,
Sun shining in on institutional carpeting
    Nervous eyes darting, listening
Silk trees in brass pots, inanimate—
Listed name bearers cross legs incessantly
    Uncross.

Magazines stacked accordion-like
Fan across antiseptic tables.
White coated nurses with heads down
Walk quickly in halls,
    Not speaking
    Not talking
Squeaking professional shoes.

Sounds of computer printers, whizzing
    Rolling, and whining
Combine with piped in generic melodies.

Chairs, mated, hook arms
To make rows of genetically
    Matched posterior vessels.

Names called in some order
Shoot patients out of their solitude
Into openings that swallow them—
    Heavy doors closing slowly
    Results pending.

Susan D. Clark (b. 1949, Alexandria, VA) traveled the world with her family as a child, and is writing children's stories about her life. She attends classes in creative writing and free-lance writing at Northern Virginia Community College. She resides in Nokesville, VA, where her family is renovating a 100 year old farmhouse.

Rhea L. Cohen

Footprints

Driftwood chip: nuance of gray sand
lit by a dragonfly. One's feet print
the lakeshore like the first finder's,
millennia before; like the Wyandot's,
three hundred summers ago.
Woman in bearskin, woman in buckskin,
    woman
in denim—watch a tenuous lifeform
affirm iridescence, pledged to wing through
another ice age. A woman upright
at water's edge makes a cradle of her arms.

Rhea L. Cohen (b. 1937, Toledo, OH) began writing poetry in 1980. A 27-year resident of Greenbelt, MD, she is a policy analyst in the Superfund program of the U.S. Environmental Protection Agency. Among her published poems, one, "Shell," won first prize in the 49th Parallel Contest of Signpost Press, in 1985, and another, "These Friends," appeared in the *New Yorker* in 1989.

Elinor Cubbage

On the Surface

White chips peel away,
Beginning their inevitable fall
    to the ground.
Wind and rain erode layer
    upon layer.
Exposing weathered clapboard.
Each time I check
Less white remains.

"It's too bad those people
Are letting their place go to pot,"
Passersby mutter.
Through unknown channels
These whispers enter my soul.
My conscience screams,
"Our historic landmark
Must be saved!
'Contentment' can be restored!"

Painstakingly constructed of
Handhewn oak, hogshair plaster,
Oyster shell mortar,
Our one hundred fifty year old
Monument has had more face lifts
Than it can remember.
Countless owners have struggled
To perform this ritual.

Break out the scrapers,
Buckets, brushes, and ladders.
Pry off the tightly sealed lids,
Roll out the speckled canvas.

Plastic surgeons grafting new life,
Brush coat upon coat,
Create a tough outer skin,
Rejuvenate your dying surface.
What medical science can never do for man
Sears Weatherbeater can do for you.

Soon your respectability will be restored
And ours with it.
Our sweat and sore muscles
A sacrifice to your immortality,
Each new coat a reminder
Of our own aging surfaces.

Elinor Cubbage (b. 1948, Laurel, DE) teaches composition and literature at Wor-Wic Community College, edits the college's student literary publication, and is advisor to the literary club. Her writing has appeared in *Modern Poetry Studies*, local newspapers, and NCTE regional newsletters. A resident of Hebron, MD, she is currently completing a doctoral degree at the University of Maryland.

Sally Dunning

Humble Perspectives

Being young and short and clear-eyed
Means having a close up view
Of your great-aunt's calves
As she bends over you with
Her spit-moistened hanky,
Redolent of bad breath,
Digging circularly into your ears,
Which are being pulled sideways
Further than they want to stretch.
And as you tap dance in pain, you
Examine her legs—all branching
Dark blue curlicues, and black
Leg hairs, flattened by her hose.

And despite her being so tall
And looking downward, which is
Why she saw your dirty ears,
("Doesn't her mother ever check
Her ears?" she tsks to herself)
She will still notice, that peeking out
From under the hem of your skirt,
Your knees are also dirty.
"It's scabs" you object.
And she says "If you would just be
Careful and watch where you are going..."

Being older, tall and soft eyed
Means not telling your grandson's mother
That you would not let him eat
That poisonous colored cereal;
And not offering to sew the shoulder seam
Of his red sweatshirt, though
This is the fourth time you've seen
That hole, and it's getting bigger.
And because you are feeling virtuous
From not doing these things,
You allow yourself to wipe his sweet face,
Sticky from breakfast hours ago,
With a paper towel and tap water.

Sally Dunning
(b. 1946, St. Louis, MO)
lives in Lake Ridge, VA.

Neal Michael Dwyer

Un Commencement

I left America. I left a black soda warm
in the black sun. I left undone
a chewed-up, spit-out morning
under Philadelphia.

I crossed a wide sea. I bit fog
and spoke beer there. Forecast called
for brown cider and blue mist
    and cold meats.

I left before I burnt. I left
singed. I left my pen. I left my
hand, mouth. I left my tongue.

I inhaled dusk-red wine over
the Mediterranean. I fished breakers
for moonlight and rose to mastlines
tapping troubadours loose from death.

I left miles of roadsigns their arrows
knowing barely the word: Tolerance.
I left the fat opinion of lately.

Neal Michael Dwyer (b. 1963, Boston, MA), studied poetry at the University of Nice, France, and at George Mason University. His poetry has been published in *Interspace, Phoebe, Vortex,* and other literary reviews in France and the U.S. Currently living in Waldorf, MD, he works as Assistant Professor of English and French at Charles County Community College. He is working on a collection of poems entitled *Two Men in the Crowded Hall.*

Margaret Edwards

Reflections

They are all gone—
the heros of my past,
so towering strong—
invincible they seemed.
I can't recall a look,
a voice; and yet
in my own image
are their faces set.

Tread Lightly

To leave a footprint
is a heavy thing:
it means you've crushed
what you have walked upon.
I guess I'd rather leave
a flower, a tree, or maybe,
in this stepped-on world,
      a song.

Margaret Edwards (b. 1932, New York, NY) has enjoyed writing for many years. Her poems have been published in various chapbooks and in past issues of *The Poet's Domain*.

Laddie Fisher

Hand and Glove

Hands grow stronger, leave behind
the baked clay image from kindergarten
as a memory of dependence dated
on a chronological track
to adulthood.
Red wooly mittens give way to leather
pockets with fingers thronged
As if the web might hold the speed
to baseball.
Browned grass-stained, sinew-hardened
fingers grasp great dreams,
add raspy work gloves,
claw the universe,
Form foundations on which career can stand
to clasp a helpmeet. With bare hand extend
the cycle borne through man's reined heart
to dare again dependency held gently
in the strength of flesh
by hand.

Laddie Fisher (b. 1920, Cincinnati, OH), a graduate of the University of Michigan and retired Public Information Officer, City of Roanoke, has published two chapbooks: *My City* (1987) and *Come Walk the Mall* (1990). Her work has appeared in numerous anthologies since 1968. Listed in *Writers in Virginia* and in *Who's Who in Writers, Editors & Poets*, she is a member of the Poetry Society of Virginia, Virginia Writers Club and Vice-President of the Roanoke Valley Branch of the National League of American Pen Women. She lives in Roanoke.

Linda Beth Fristoe

The Prince who Loved Me Darkly

He walked toward the world
I wandered with my unicorn
and silently studied
my secrets in the mist
until one winter day
he captured me
while I lay
cradling my unicorn,
its horn thrust
against my thigh gently.
He brought to our bridal bower
a golden fox with glittering eyes
and planted purple passion
in my furrowed garden
where he taught me
to taste darkness sweetly.
Spiriting me to a castle,
he locked the gates
and burned invitations
to other balls
while he wove a silken tapestry
of tales believed too soon
and understood too late.
From my lonely tower
I awakened one year
to the siren song
of a mermaid in the moat.
Elysian freedom fields called
and I stole away
toward the night
wearing only the footprint
of my prince
across my heart darkly.

Linda Beth Fristoe (b. 1958, Terra Alta, WV) studied poetry at the University of Virginia, where she earned her master's degree. She presently teaches creative writing and language arts seminars in Front Royal, VA, where she resides. Her work appeared in *English Journal, Midwest Poetry Review, Virginia Country, Deros, Midway Review,* and numerous other poetry magazines.

Linda Beth Fristoe

Lotus Flower*

For Carrie Virginia Bowen
2-21-89 / 2-21-89

Destined never to be
with us long enough
for dolls and daydreams
or summers of silver rains,
a fragile flower
arose with the sun
and slept with the moon.
Blossoming briefly,
she closed gently,
like a sleepy lotus
cradling a soul,
to soar across rainbows,
past the silent stars
toward a moonbeam home
where she waits
wearing wings.

(**Lotus* symbolizes nascent life or first appearance
equated with the heart and final revelation.)

Gertrude Gunther

Music

I drop beet seeds—
of musical notes
the heads—
into the soil
along a line
of garden staff
and conceive a monotone
subject to possibilities
of tempo.

The Polite Parlor

query's red
path to the queried
like the sun's
from horizon
to cut glass
sparks glittering
response.

Gertrude Gunther (b. 1911, Mexico City, Mexico) studied poetry at Barnard College. Living on Virginia's Eastern Shore in Onancock the past twenty-three years, she celebrates the region with poetry booklets, among them *Pussyfooting through Nature*. Her poems have appeared in *The Christian Science Monitor*, the *Anthology of Poems by Member Poets*, Poetry Society of Virginia (1985), and *The Poet's Domain*, Vols. 1 though 6.

JoAnn Hartman

The Golden Gate

There ain't never been a job
Like the Golden Gate—
Top pay in hard times,
Cold to the bone,
Wild winds and tides.

Never was higher than the garage roof,
Then the Golden Gate.
Myself against the bridge—
Busted my teeth,
Lost my footing,
Fell halfway to Hell,
Flipped three times
And hit the net.
Eight weeks in the hospital.

Sell shoestrings
Cause you'll never get off alive.
A gust of wind
And we all got scared
Cause the safety net went down
And the tide was out.

Why didn't I quit?
I love the fog,
The smell of bourbon.
We raised Hell on the bridge;
Some were killed or maimed,
Quit or fell,
Fifty years ago.
Its got my fingerprints—
The Golden Gate.

JoAnn Hartman (b. 1933, Watertown, NY), reading specialist in Loudoun County, VA, makes her poetry debut in this edition. A resident of Waterford, VA, she has been a member of the Poetry Society of Virginia for many years.

Barbara McKay Hewin

Nightmare Alice

Now the ancient body trembled,
strained against the desk to stand
as another class assembled
under motion of her hand.

Once again she watched them coming,
golden faces touched with grime,
and her heart grew tired with drumming
and her soul grew dark with time.

Endless coming, endless going,
endless names with endless looks,
human thought with braces showing,
throwing down its endless books;

Bread that must have yeast to raise it,
silver thread that needs a loom,
beauty without voice to praise it
streaming by into the room.

And she thought, "How pure the laughter,
rich and sweet with unspent years;
oh, my seed—my life hereafter—
make it worth my lonely tears.

"Make it worth the long frustration,
worth the deep inhuman cold,
worth the pain of inspiration
derelict and growing old.

"Do not leave me just a creature
standing barren by the tomb;
let this aging ugly teacher
bring your talents into bloom!"

Then as distant bells entreated—
grumpy old Miss Allison
sounded thunder and repeated,
"Quiet! Turn to Lesson One!"

Barbara McKay Hewin (b. 1927, New York, NY)—poet and homemaker—won a 1st Place award in the Virginia A.A.U.W. poetry contest. Her poems have appeared in *The Poet's Domain* Vols. 1 through 6, and in *Poetic Voices of America*. She is listed in *Writers in Virginia* and continues writing from her home in Kingsmill-on-the-James, Williamsburg, VA.

Jane H. Hu

Tea House

The moon was pale,
    The lights in the Ginza were dazzling.

A transient sojourner,
    Under a lamplight alone,
    Let the smoke and mist drift in the air.

Opening a writing paper on the table,
    I had no need for bitter wine,
    Only the fragrance of tea.

Several volumes of poetry,
    And one pen
    Accompanied me around the world.

Jane H. Hu (b. 1940, Chekiang, China), is a Health Scientist Administrator at the National Institutes of Health. Her poems were published in the *American Poetry Anthology,* 1990; *Selected Works of World's Best Poets,* 1991; *The Best Poems of the '90s,* 1992. She also published Chinese poems in leading Chinese newspapers in Taiwan and in the United States. She lives in Potomac, MD.

Nancy Stuart Hundley

The Way Home

We dreaded the rain,
(It was late night)
Slow driving the way home,
Patches of fog coming in,
Like gray cotton balls
Bouncing up from the road
Making the night eery still.
The car hummed us along.
We were dry and feeling love.
We tuned our thoughts,
Chatted without the radio on,
The sounds of rain pleasant and gentle
As we toward each other,
Dreams spinning in the rain.

Nancy Stuart Hundley (b. 1934, Richmond, VA), has sold several poems to magazines and has had others published in little magazines and anthologies. She lives in Boydton, VA.

Rosalie S. Jennings

The Mayor's Shield

Beside the Council entrance on mirrored glass
The clouds of sunset warm the mayor's eyes.
He faces west to let the softness in.
The sun's deserting closes out each day,
No final resignation. His is the job
To give the Council notice, say goodbye!

Or will it be that good intent can keep
A balance with the jostle of dissent?
And if there comes no argument tonight,
Why can't it wait? Perhaps his own fatigue
Has thinned assurance down until he seeks
Defense against the "S's" they have cast:
Senile! Slow! Stubborn! Stupid! And yet
They know how much he loves the town,
     how much
He hopes for unity to grow. But now,
Like dying day, it dims and loses warmth.

Against the pinch of nervous wait, he lights
His pipe and paces up and down the walk.
His whispered voice repeats the careful words
Rehearsed at home—a sudden swoop of chill
And something snaps—these words he
     cannot use!
What blessing can there be in calling quits?
He stomps to chase the cold and faces east:
Orion's rise is like the swell he feels
Against the hurt—a valiant shield regained
To keep him in the ranks of selfless men.

Rosalie S. Jennings (b. 1917, Woodstock, VA) is a member of Shenandoah Valley Writers' Guild, conducts poetry workshops, and frames her illumined original poems for art shows. She lives in Edinburg, VA.

Avah Johnson

Epicedium

Nothing is heavier
than the emptiness you left.

It is deeper than the primal gurgle,
wider than the entire estates
of heaven, hell, and tomorrow,
those worn-out worlds
we yawned about so mindlessly.

We knew they were only a breath away
but never could have imagined
the chill, the chasm of that breath.

Nor could I have known
the compelling focus of your absence.
I can't remember what I used to do
—or why,
nor can I imagine the future.
Each minute is tortured and contorted.

You took only what was yours;
but to have my very heart buried
leaves me with no beat
to regulate my step.

Yet, your light lingers—brighter
than any cluster of galaxies,
highlighting every crevice of the past,
parts I had never seen before,
parts I had *never* seen before.

Avah Johnson (b. 1925, Springfield, KY) has had poems published in *The Poet's Domain*, *Rye Bread Rising*, *The New York Times*, the Poetry Society of Virginia's *Anthology of Poems*, *Oriole*, The Anthology of the Maryland State Poetry Society, *Haiku*, Washington Poets Association and other journals. She lives in McLean, VA.

Agnes Nasmith Johnston

Appalachian Trails

Fingering an acorn,
we ask questions,
search forest and stream,
peer at trout,
gather dandelion green.

Who are we?
Scot, Cherokee, African...

Mist veils mountain ranges
as we shout, our echoes
vibrating through the valley.

Now, tracking footprints
of our kin, we knead
new dreams, bake bread

and waltz
in dogwood spring.

Agnes Nasmith Johnston (b. 1921, Huchow, China) graduated from Shanghai American School and the University of Rochester, worked for the State Department as a research analyst and was a Foreign Service spouse. She has had poems in every volume of *The Poet's Domain*. Her first book of poetry, *Beyond the Moongate* (Lotus Press) came out in 1987 with another printing in 1989. She continues to write poems about her return to China in 1988 and has recently been published in *Black Buzzard Review*, *Hollins Critic*, and *The China Connection*. She is listed in *Writers in Virginia*.

Cincinnati Girl

You laugh
in lilt of tones
up and down
like the green hills
of your city
above the rollicking river.

You've traveled—
spun fantasies—
tales of prince
and princess,
child and dog,
kittens rolling yarn.

How many ridges
have we climbed,
snowflakes tongued
in winter storm?

Agnes Nasmith Johnston

Mist shrouds the valley.
Trains hiss
a departure warning.

I touch your hand
cold as white jade
for your final mountain.

Flyers

Airing
my caged brown bird
in the courtyard, I know
he does not chirp the early songs
of spring.

I wish
that I could fly
high among bamboo stands
to taste the wind's cool teasing on
my skin.

My sleeves
cling like soft wings
yet I cannot lift up
to skim the rice fields of distant
valleys.

Fog clouds
rove on mountains
where *hua-mei* songbirds trill
in their temples of green forest
secrets.

Morning
golds my bird cage
and I open the latch.
My bird darts above garden pools,
circles,

perches
on my hand, flaps
his brown wings and I feel
our hearts soaring in harmony.
We sing.

Jean P. Klotzbach

My Mother Said

Life is too short for bitterness,
Much too long for hate,
Cast them aside, enjoy life's ride,
Before it is too late.

Away with *If, Why Didn't I,*
Take up *I Can, I'll Try, I Will,*
Positive thinking, no more soul shrinking
Before you're "over the hill."

Open your mind and eager arms,
Begin to change today...
You will be thrilled when they are filled
With the joys you've been chasing away.

You Are Old

When you no longer thrill at a sunset,
Are not awed as a new foal is born,
Do not weep at the heartbreak of others,
Cannot taste with delight fresh-picked corn,

If you don't like a kitten's small paw on your arm,
And a babe's cry brings only disgust,
Well, then you're OLD, lady, and maybe, just maybe,
We're damn glad you're NOT one of us!

Jean P. Klotzbach (b. 1921, Buffalo, NY) has travelled extensively with career and family and presently resides in Columbia, MD. She enjoys writing poetry and short stories and looks forward to each day's new experiences in living.

Jean P. Klotzbach

Memory

Old folks seem to hold their memories close.
I wish I could forget some of mine.
When I was a "teen" I would sit and dream,
Not give a thought about time.

God, I could run as fast as a deer,
Walk without stopping each mile,
I could dance all night till the sun came up
And still run into work with a smile.

I had a shape that could make men quake,
Skin the color of an English rose.
Here I am, now, a size 38
The skin's full of age spots and moles.

Rode the wildest horse like a cossack,
I loved life and grabbed out for more.
Now I'm 72 and the old "bod" says no,
What am I still around for?

Please leave a few memories, if you will,
I'll enjoy life the best way I can.
Maybe I'll come up lucky.
Even might find me a man!

Mary Rose Knapp

Consumed

The courtship was gradual.
You wrapped around me
gentle and slow,
Squeezing me tighter
with attention and charm.
Then the day came;
I said, "I do."
You swallowed me whole
and I became you.
You've been the centerpiece
of my life:
Your name is Husband;
mine is wife.

Mary Rose Knapp
(b. 1964, Fairfax, VA)
makes her poetry debut
in this edition. She lives
in Dale City, VA.)

Olive S. Lanham

Dance on the Dunes

Wind curves beach grasses
        to sway and bend like dancers—
        feet anchored in sand.

Destination

Our lives began
    and still begin
in that single shining second
    when you looked at me
        and into me—
and we both knew.

It all was quite decided
    even then, before we were
        acquaintances, or friends,
    and long before we stumbled through
        the rituals of life.

What was to come
    held laughter,
        joy and tears,
    but these would not
        and could not change our
            course,
for buried in our deepest hearts
    we knew
        that we had recognized each other—
        we were home.

Olive S. Lanham (b. 1924, Soochow, China) studied at Shanghai American School and Duke. Her work has appeared in Vols. 5 and 6 of *The Poet's Domain*. She has written short stories, and a 3-act play in poetry. She enjoys setting her poems to music. She is a member of Tomoka Poets, the Daytona chapter of Florida State Poets' Association, and the National League of American Pen Women.

Mary Antil Lederman

Art is long, and Time is fleeting...
"A Psalm of Life,"
Henry Wadsworth Longfellow

Footprints of the Soul

(dedicated to fellow poet Bess Gresham,
who died June 28, 1992.)

Sand castles, like their crafters' footprints,
    will last, alas, but one short day.
They—like our mortal dreams and lives—
    by relentless Time are washed away.
But the all merciful Creator,
    to mitigate Man's mortal state,
Shares with his human creations
    his own divine power to create;

And *Homines sapiens* empowered
    live for millennia to be
Through the beauty crafted in their lives
    in all its totality.
The soul's essence breathes, communicates
    after the human hull is shed.
The artist—sculptor, painter, poet—
    through his Art is never dead.

Mary Antil Lederman (b. 1925, Los Angeles, CA), a retired foreign language teacher, served 20 years as department head at Albemarle High School in Charlottesville. She earned a *magna cum laude* B.A. degree from Syracuse University and a master's degree at the University of Virginia. In addition to national prizes, she has won numerous Poetry Society of Virginia prizes since 1989. Her work has appeared in *Albemarle* magazine, *The Observer*, VRTA *Broadcast*, *Poetic Voices of America*, *Treasured Poems of America*, 1990, 1991, *Orphic Lute* and Vols. 2 through 6 of *The Poet's Domain*.

Mary Antil Lederman

Let us, then, be up and doing,
With a heart for any fate...
"A Psalm of Life,"
Henry Wadsworth Longfellow.)

Sunny Side Out!

A smile is an instant face-lift—
    check your mirror—this is so!
It's magically cosmetic
    not to let your sadness show.

Without one a face looks grumpy—
    especially when on in years!
A smile chases psychic storm clouds
    like sunshine when it appears.

It's a non-prescriptive tonic
    that we can all afford
And makes us better company,
    inviting mutual accord.

That it takes fewer muscles than
    frowning does is really true,
And leaves one with more energy
    for the things one has to do.

It is the one adornment
    that, often worn, never wears out—
Keeping stormy weather inside
    and cheerful sunshine without.

"Let a smile be your umbrella"
    is not just a tired cliché...
It prevents dampening spirits
    from dousing a sunny day.

So, don't let inner cloudbursts
    darken everywhere you go.
Even when you're consumed with care,
    keep smiling—who needs to know?

Joan Leotta

Grand Canyon Visit

I took pictures
of us—
father, mother, son and daughter—
so we would
remember
the colors and our good time.

My daughter
bought
earrings at the stands
so her ears
would hear
the canyon's rhythms always.

My husband
bought books
to learn more
about the wonders
we had seen and missed
at the canyon.

My son
spit
into the canyon,
so the canyon
would not
forget *him*.

Joan Leotta (b. 1948, Pittsburgh, PA), professional storyteller and writer, lives in Burke, VA. She has performed her repertoire of original tales and adaptations of folklore widely, including, at the Kennedy Center. Her book, *Writing Techniques for Hotel Managers*, came out in 1992. Her poetry, fiction, and non-fiction for children and adults is published in many magazines. She teaches storytelling and writing non-fiction and poetry. She is listed in *Writers in Virginia*.

Joseph Lewis

Starry Night

The stars look good tonight sometime
in November toward the end of the year;

they all seem so clear as one forgets
debts and disasters on tomorrow's news.

One wants to be the philosopher who sees them
as never before, the most sought for prize,

hoping to find the history of the world
in their scattered symmetries. Then to pass

under a window where the laughter of a girl
gets carried away in the autumn breeze,

past the trees already stripped bare
down to their most essential form so we

can calculate when the next winter comes,
reminding ourselves of our final fall,

how yellow leaves seem the right metaphor,
walking under a clear sky full of stars.

Joseph Lewis (b. 1948, Pittsburgh, PA) lives in Williamsburg, VA. His poetry appeared in Vol. 5 of *The Poet's Domain*.

Harriet Campbell Little

The Silent Seconds
(Virginia—1622)

He should have been anywhere,
he thought, but not here—
in the wilderness.
He should have been at Cambridge
scribbling notes
with his blue feathered quill pen
or in his chamber listening to the ticking
of his small French clock,
but not here—
locked in a frozen stance and stare
waiting for the awesome arrow
to pierce the air
and him.

Harriet Campbell Little (b. 1923, Richmond, VA) studied poetry at Suffolk University in Boston and at Shenandoah College and Conservatory in Winchester. A former member of the Poetry Society of Virginia, her poetry has appeared in Vols. 3, 4, and 5 of *The Poet's Domain*. She lives at Piping Tree Gardens near Beaverdam, VA.

Katie Goldstein Lorber

South Florida I

It's beautiful here. Yes?
But in the nights I dream from
the camps. You know from
the camps?

(Like the ancient mariner the old man walks
    about the pool, the sun hot, singeing the
    numbers on his arm.)

It's very nice here. You know?
Who would think of such a place in
the camps. You know from
the camps?

(He came from the village next to my father's
    village; his numbers and the sun begin to
    pierce my arm.

Old man, the tale is in my blood.
I know from the camps.

South Florida II

I glide into the cadence of the Bronx—
sentences structured convolutedly,
sung loudly punctuated by
laughter and hands.
Forgotten words return—my mother tongue
truly draws the world lovingly,
depicts the soul the heart
of all that matters.
Such words are rich and round with
memories.

My children are boring—they speak
    correctly—
they do not sing.

Katie Goldstein Lorber (b. 1929, Bronx, NY) attended the High School of Music and Art (for music) and the City College of New York. She lived with her engineer husband and children in Lahore, W. Pakistan, where she published *Oh So Young, I'll Never Die*, a book of paintings and poems. In the states, she taught emotionally disturbed children. She sold paintings and published poems in several anthologies, including *The Crucible, N.C. Poetry Society*, and *Chazon*. She lives in Columbia, MD.

Michael Hugh Lythgoe

Aubade for Archaeology

> Art is long, and time is fleeting.
> —Henry Wadsworth Longfellow,
> "A Psalm of Life"

We hear the wind chimes ring and feel
The fall, the first gust of Autumn,
An early chill, a cold front's omen.
The clear, lessening light's ordeal
Is our reminder of the length
Of shadows we share,
The strength of our belief
In the minstrel's power
To heal with his lyre and his rhymes,
To leave everlasting voice-prints in our
   minds.

If art is long, and time is fleeting,
Resurrect the bare and ruined choirs!
Learn to chant again the hours,
Or join the diggers in their search for
   meaning.
Let us unearth the ancient tombs
Preserving signs of life, the lasting marks—
Pieces of a people's spirit—shards of poems,
Pigment-stories peeled from cave walls,
   ink-black
Brush strokes on scrolls of rice paper,
Priceless sounds: the first music from a
   Moor's guitar.

Deficits deepen; the coin of the realm declines.
To spend, not bank, the currency of the brisk
   wind
In calligraphy, or breath, is best. Imagine
The tinkling tones of the wind chimes'
   rhymes.
Footprints left in hasty sands will hardly last
Long enough for the archaeologists to find,
When they sift through our solid waste.
Press our prints as leaves in pages of molten
   slime,
Minting lava-like fossils for our legacy,
Molding fate from clay of grace: creativity.

Michael Hugh Lythgoe (b. 1941, Evansville, Indiana) lives in Gainesville, VA. His poems have appeared in Vols. 4, 5, and 6 of *The Poet's Domain*. He has recently read his poems at the 1992 Eastern Regional Conference on Christianity and Literature at Messiah College in PA, Abercrombie Book Store in Manassas, and at the Nokesville Mini Library. One of his poems was selected as an Honorable Mention winner in The Sixth Annual John David Johnson Memorial Poetry Competition (1992). He studied with the poet and essayist, John Haines, in a community writers workshop sponsored by the Jenny McKean Moore Fund for Writers at George Washington University. He has poems forthcoming in *The Eclectic Literary Forum* (ELF), and The Eastern Caribbean Institute anthology of ten poets.

Michael Hugh Lythgoe

A Winter Cure
(for Mildred Gay)

As snow descends today in Maine,
Mounting drifts climb to window pane,

Memory-flecks swirl in my mind.
I dream back to another winter time—

When my mother held my sister
Down on kitchen table, for the doctor

Who operated on the two-year-old;
He then prescribed for her the cold:

A healing time outside in icy tent.
In the weather a young woman bent

Over a crib beneath chilled canvas;
Inside wood burns and smoke rises

Up as puffs of prayers. From inside
We worry about what's outside,

The incisions in young lungs,
Why surgeon speaks with gothic tongue?

He frightened me with his medical case.
Said babies hatched in that black place.

He threatened me, saying he would
Put me in the bag—dark as woods.

I hid in fear of being his prisoner.
Cured sister served fifty years as Post Master.

In harsh New England the doctor
Healed then with a certain terror.

Adults often tell stories to scare.
Good can come from discipline and fear.

The Poet's Domain

Joan Maloof

The Sound Water Makes As It Pours Through the Alphabet of Names

What are these memories
in us
that know flight?
Why are the angels gathering
again
this century?
And the birds wing
with every translation
of sound, season or sun.
The leaving and the coming home:
curvaceous chaos.
And a motion, too,
we cannot see.
Perhaps time folds
and your body
is once again
on top of me.

Joan Maloof (b. 1956, Wilmington, DE) is a naturalist living in a riverside farmhouse near the small town of Quantico, on Maryland's Eastern Shore. She has a special interest in plants, both wild and cultivated.

Joan Maloof

Cycles

She knows the time to sit and wait.
Tomorrow the first weed will erupt with
    bloom.
Maybe the next she will walk the tideline
on the damp mud, when the water is low,
looking for the prints bearing three toes,
savoring some solitary treasure
before the moon comes round
returning all to the sea.
Soon it will be time for the waxwings
to bring their bright beaks back to the
    orchard.
Let's cover this bowl and let the yeast rise.
We will wait to see what fine thing tries us
    next,
what fine surprise. Some ancient softening,
perhaps a pair of oak brown eyes;
or new life tumbling inside.
A life that's cycle tied.

Alice Shoger Mawdsley

One Way

They wanted to do it our way
With a Statue of Liberty, free speech and press,
In a spring when young hopes turned to freedom,
While television cameras made them heroes.

But it could only be done their way
In a hundred-acre square of concrete monuments,
Without a Bunker Hill or a Paul Revere,
Singing, talking, hungering for their cause.

Then a night of a thousand blazing guns
Tanks against bare flesh, killing daughters and sons,
Hopes crushed, crimson death, hate unleashed,
The old man said it had to end his way.

I Shall Weep for You

I shall weep for you
When earth's black hope turns green
Under April's soft rain
And bright sun brings sacred life to birth.

I shall weep for you
When blazing geraniums burst forth
Beside your now closed door,
Remembering soft summer breezes against your face.

I shall weep for you
When golden wheat and corn
Shine against the blue chillness of the sky
And Fall's brilliant tapestry weaves forth.

I shall weep for you
When Winter's white covers dead earth's black embrace
And I am finally aware
That you have really gone.

Alice Shoger Mawdsley (b. 1948, Aurora, IL), English and drama professor, has published poetry in various journals. Teaching and traveling in Egypt and England, she is currently working on a book on Ancient Egyptian Drama.

James L. Mawdsley

To a Friend

What have we
done to you
all you wanted
was to be a friend
give
teach us love
that would give
us the way give
us a way
and we kill for you
and condemn for you
an eye
for an eye
(foreign eye)
and your eyes
drown away
at the thought
that we thought
that this
is what you taught.

James L. Mawdsley (b. 1975, Minneapolis, MN), high school senior, has won numerous essay and poetry contests. His poetry has been published in the *Piedmont Literary Review*. Currently entered in the National Merit Scholarship competition, he achieved a perfect 800 score on the SAT verbal test.

Jonathan R. Mawdsley

To the author of the article "What the world will be like in the year 1984"

I know
I'm looking
with hindsight
at your foresight,
but it seems more
than just fifty
short years ago
you dared dream
of a future
unburdened by

Dichlorodiphenyltrichloroethane
polychlorobiphenyls
and thermonuclear waste.

But you didn't know then
and I still don't know now
that what we don't know
won't hurt us.
Will it?

Jonathan R. Mawdsley (b. 1972, Minneapolis, MN), Harvard University student, won the student prize at the Poetry Society of Virginia Workshop and has had numerous articles published on entomology. A National Merit Scholar, his special interest is beetles. The last six summers he has studied insects in England and Belgium.

Dorothy W. Millner

On the Stairs

Neighbors for years
we pass on the stairs
nod
not aware of each other.

One day she says,
"I lost my job.
My children worry,
but I'll get another."

Months later I see
couches and chairs
descending the stairs.
"We are moving to my mother's,"
she smiles brightly,
fear in her eyes
like a trapped rabbit.

People come and go.
We see them every day,
we don't give a second thought
until one day
empty spaces on the stairs
resonate loudly.

Dorothy W. Millner (b.   , Pittsburgh, PA) graduated from Sarah Lawrence college, earned a Ph.D. degree from The Graduate Center: City University of New York, and taught literature at Pace University, Pleasantville, NY. She moved to Alexandria, VA, in 1975 to work for the Federal government on various management analysis and writing projects. Now retired, she teaches at the Learning and Retirement Institute, George Mason University. She is a member of the Poetry Society of Virginia.

Robert R. Montgomery

Robert R. Montgomery (b. 1923, Quantico, VA), practiced cardiology in Bethesda, MD, until he retired in 1985. He wrote many articles for professional and boating journals, but now concentrates on writing poetry in his home on Wilton Creek in Hartfield, VA. His poems have appeared in *The Poet's Domain* volume 6, *Pleasant Living*, and *Southside Sentinel*, and have won prizes in the Chesapeake Writers' Conference in 1991 and 1992.

Diogenes

The ancient lantern-bearer sought
A man whose word would stand the test
Of careful scrutiny, and rest
All doubts, reduce mistrust to nought,
A man whose truth could not be bought
Whose every spoken word possessed
No lie, covert or manifest,
Disguised as tact or afterthought.
Today his shade pursues the search—
Two thousand years, still incomplete—
He lights the face of kings of men,
Of candidates and priests of church,
But finds in each some deep deceit
And lifts his lamp again, again.

Lost Toddler

The baby came and nestled
into their lives aboard
the little vessel.

She giggled and learned to sit
and stand alone within
the cockpit.

It was her place, her playpen
when she began to crawl.
And then

She learned to walk and climb
up to the cockpit seats.
One final time

She toddled toward the side
and finished childhood in
the ebbing tide.

David J. Partie

Looking at a Photograph of Stephen Crane, 1894

Yellowed with time and faded with sun,
sitting on a rooftop in New York,
you gaze into the hazy afternoon,
frozen forever with arm on knee,
a prisoner of celluloid,
abstracted in white and grey.
The letters on the buildings on the left
are obliterated or sliced by beams,
indecipherable hieroglyphs
as inscrutable as your mind,
hidden under your bowler hat.
The camera was a liar,
its eye as blind as Cyclops'
to claim that you who had broken
through water in the open boat,
in Greece had bent bullets into words,
and in your dreams had defied
the red gods of war,
were ever mute and motionless
under a colorless New York sky.
This ghostly photograph now
has more substance than your bones.
Your rooftop has crumbled too,
buried under earth and decades,
vanished with carriages and gaslights.
But this image,
like light from some ancient star,
has just reached me.
This mysterious thread
connecting both our worlds
may be all that is left of you and then—
except for your breathing books.

David J. Partie (b. 1944, Detroit, MI) won the Poetry Society of Virginia's Karma Deane Ogden Prize in 1991 for his poem "For the Suicide of Hart Crane" and was a first prize winner in the 1991 Lynchburg Poetry Festival. He received his Ph. D. in Comparative Literature from the University of Southern California. He lives in Lynchburg, VA, and teaches German and English at Liberty University, where he also serves as Chairman of the Department of Modern Languages.

Patricia Royal Perkinson

50th Reunion
or
If I Hadn't Been Too Vain to Wear My Bifocals, I Could Make Out That Nametag!

Patricia Royal Perkinson (b. 1925, Middlesex Co., VA), former Secretary of the Commonwealth of Virginia, aide to Governor Mills Godwin, *Richmond Times-Dispatch* columnist and Virginia Press Women president, resumed poetry writing after retiring to an antebellum family home at Topping. She is a contributing editor of *Pleasant Living* magazine, member of the Virginia Writers Club, and active volunteer on the American Cancer Society's national board, the Rappahannock Community College board, and boards of several local organizations.

"Remember you?
Why, of *course* I do!
How could you think
I'd misplace *you*?

"Those were the days,
Now weren't they then?
We shared all the best.
Great to see you again!"

Mmmm—

Physique all but gone,
New chins to spare,
Belt sub-equator,
No trace of hair.

Subtract several decades,
Blend in some tan,
A full-blown toupee…
Oh, who *was* that man?

Darn!

Who was that fellow?
I haven't a clue.
Just hope he wasn't one
I gave my heart to!

Tad Phipps

Color Blind

Put the ocean's Water
and the sky's Sun
together
Get the tree's Leaves.

Mother says it is green,
so be it.
For I respect and believe in her.
It is green.

But how do I know my green
isn't her ocean's Water,
or her sky's Sun?
For I cannot see through her greens.

Put the tree's Leaves,
and the ocean's Water
together
Get the sky's Sun.

Tad Phipps (b. 1972, Fort Hood, TX) won his first competition in poetry at the age of ten. He continues to work on his first book, *Controlled Chaos*. Raised in Southwest Virginia, he is a student at Virginia Polytechnic Institute and State University and resides in Blacksburg, VA.

Richard Raymond, III

Beach Rover

The sea is calm...tonight.
That "melancholy, long, withdrawing roar"
returned some time ago, brimming with faith
    and fight.
If only we, who paddle by the shore,
could be as cocksure as these multitudes,
these deep and driving tides who brook of no
    delay,
no pleas, like Cromwell's, to imagine they
might be mistaken—they are *stuffed* with
    certitudes.

I stroll along the beach
where great waves flung dead timbers out of
    reach.
The wet sand slows my steps. I stoop and
    write
a line of verse, my finger as a pen,
black letters, under pale moonlight,
(will it be here, when I look back again?).

The tide of faith, it seems, is on the flood,
millions are marching, moving—who knows
    where?
A great unending pour
of people, waving placards in the air,
shaking of flags and fists, silent no more.
When streams collide, these waters bloat with
    blood.

Orators spout like sea-spray, windy fogs
drift in, and partisans applaud the
    demagogues'
sonorities, as music to their ears:
"...abortion...equal rights...unequal pay...
homeless...pollution, peace, the Pentagon...
creationism...race..." whoever's in the way
of *their* parade had best begone!
Ignorant armies, yet—now armed with
    sharpened spears.

My naked toes trudge through the sands of
    time,

Richard Raymond, III (b. 1930, Cambridge, NY), a graduate of U.S. Naval Academy, served in the U.S. Marine Corps. His poems have appeared in *Army Times*, *Leatherneck*, *Infantry*, and *Naval Institute Proceedings*, and three previous issues of *The Poet's Domain*. An engineering technician, he has won three 1st place awards in the 1992 World Order of Narrative & Formalist Poets and has had four poems in the 1961 Civil War anthology *From Sumter to Appomattox*.

Richard Raymond, III

a dimpled track along the naked shingle of
    the world,
avoiding bands of slime—
the sea is, for the moment, calm, the moon is
    bright.
I glance behind once, and behold,
a long wave licks my letters out of sight.

Seasons

Summer on the hills,
Deep-green flaglets fluttering
Semaphores of joy.

Scarlet, amber leaves
Fading, shading into brown—
Leaves and lives scale down.

Winter wraps our world
In whorls of white. But will seeds
Germinate, come spring?

April stirs dull roots.
I will *not* be disheartened.
There *will* be lilacs.

Fred F. Richardson

My Uncle's Shoes

1

From a corner of my parent's closet,
under dust and memories and shadows
of how things change and are forgotten
over sixty some years, my sister handed me
a pair of old brown shoes jolting me
nearly to divulge, to confide in her; but I put
 them down,
not exactly sure those were the shoes,
not knowing just how to begin.
They weren't straight in my mind, like a
 photograph
having faded with time, and perhaps I was wrong.

2

Still, the old leather shoes are in my mind,
and that jolting feeling
does not go away, and
I find myself remembering that night,
although a lifetime has passed
leaving everyone there dead but me,
the night I watched the Ku Klux Klan beat a man.
I believe it was December of 1931.
I sat listening to my uncle explain Eastern
 Shore winters
to the men gathered in old man West's
 general store.
He was leaning against the counter,
the men gathered round grinning
to his theory of the bay and the ocean and the
 wind.
How they chorused in "idn't it" when he
 declared it's God's country.
He kicked my stool and slapped my leg hard
 laughing,
and told my dad it was time for the little man
 to go home to bed.
Dad sent me home to help mom while he
 cleaned up for Mr. West.
My uncle and the others went off laughing
 into the mild December night.

3

It's odd thinking of my uncle back then.

Fred F. Richardson (b. 1950, Machipongo, VA) resides on Jacobas Creek in Northampton County, where he teaches English and math. His works have appeared in *Green's Magazine* in Canada and the University of Virginia *Voices*. Currently, he is working on a collection of poems based on the people and nature of the Eastern Shore of Virginia.

Fred F. Richardson

Over the years I have dealt with many men
    like him
and have grown increasingly puzzled as to
    their hold on people,
still I know this: You have to oppose them if
    you refuse to follow them.
Not once, but always. He had told my father
    to send me home,
and for a moment the room did not move,
his words squeezed the souls of everyone in
    the room,
and my father knew it was the moment,
to do otherwise would only delay the
    inevitable.
Resigned, he had sent me home.
I didn't understand the moment then, only now
looking back see the truth,
and want to go back, to knowingly refuse,
to be twenty years older and six feet tall,
and defy him.

4

We lived next door atop the Redbird Gas
    Station.
I had lingered outside the general store
waiting for dad to lock up,
to hear his jingling keys,
my signal to run ahead home before he saw me,
when I saw torches up the road
bobbing in the night, a river of lights
coming towards town.
I slid down in the shadows beside the station
as angry voices became hooded men
in white sheets.
I watched them pass old man West's store,
cross the street,
drag a drunkened waterman out of his house,
tie him to a cross,
and bull-whip him until he was blood.
They told him never spend his money
on whiskey or women or cards again,
to give his money to his wife,
to feed and clothe his children,
or they'd be back.
In the wavering torch light
they cut him down and set fire to the cross.
Scared and bleeding he fell at their feet.
That's when I saw those shoes,
the brown leather shoes of my uncle
kick the waterman and lead the men away.

Evelyn Ritchie

Ordered Pair, Graphed (x+y=1)

I, abscissa; you, ordinate—
Together one, we meet and mate
At the halfpoint, both rational,
The level and the vertical.

If I diminish, would you fill
The larger fraction in good will?
If you were sinking, would you let
Me boost the values in my set?

Dear y, I your elastic x
Can stoop and leap, would stand or flex,
Would share with you domain and range.
Let us add up through any change.

And shun the gaping negative
Under the stasis where we live,
Lest, racked by an irrational cost,
Our life's equation should be lost.

Ringing In My Ears

Call it the tide of silence, lapped
Circlets of sand
Round a once-peopled city. Stand
Still and be wrapped.

The music of the spheres, perhaps?
Night-radio
Now plucking chance sidereal flow
From heavenly taps?

Could it be my pursuing past,
A Furies-swarm
Confused by detours, holding harm
For one strong blast?

Evelyn Ritchie (b. 1927, Criders, VA) is the author of *Hickory Sled*, a book of verse. She has won various awards for her poems. A member of the Poetry Society of Virginia, she has contributed to the *New Virginia Review*, *Poet Lore*, the *Midwest Review*, *Blue Unicorn*, and *Fiesta*, and is a contributing editor for *Virginia Country*. An educational missionary to Korea and a lifelong teacher, she makes her home in Richmond, VA, where she is working on a new volume of poems and a book for children.

Evelyn Ritchie

Call it the wind on the lee side,
The murmuring
Unraining clouds that mass and cling
Above the tide.

Waiting Up For My Son

In a corner house upstairs
Tossing, I monitor each turn
That might be motor slowing,
Muffled stop, and soft slam
To end my vigil.

When he locks the door
Beneath my window, my blood lowers
In both eyes. I dismiss the watch.

As he bounds the stairway,
I re-assess my lookout:
Useless as old greeting cards,
Thankless as vaccination,
Temporary as dinner,
Controlled as the Mississippi.
The brain concedes folly,
Forcing the heart to concur,
And only the gut twangs
Its phantom twinge
Begun in nine-month constriction,
And holds the spasm
Until it rests again
In dying fall of tires.

Leslie Sands

House for Sale

Who wants to buy the house
perched on the rim of a wooded ravine?
It comes complete with ancient trees
and a symphony of bird songs.
The front door's framed
with burnt red of Japanese maple
and tiger-orange daylilies.
Inside's a baked-in fragrance
of gingerbread and rose petals.

Three girls were raised in its
four tiny rooms when times were hard.
Santa Claus rode up the half-circle lane
on top of a fire truck to greet
children who crackled wrapping paper
in their shyly waving hands.

Its kitchen, a place for kids to nestle
at the table with mugs of cocoa
after hours of exploring among
Mayapple and Jack-in-the-Pulpit,
searching for the patch of quicksand
where it was said a little boy fell in
and never was seen again.

The dining room still echoes
with the jumbled voices
of countless family repasts,
complete with acclaim
to the blushing cook
and shrill arguments over
the crisp browness of the drumstick,
its meat divided at last by some
Solomon of a parent.

The house's owner no longer owns
the functions of her body.
Her mind travels meandering roads
no one else can follow.
She lives in an adjustable bed,
surrounded by the odor of disinfectant.
They say she won't be back.

Leslie Sands (b. 1949, Trenton, NJ) currently lives in Smithfield, VA. She is a teacher of English at Warwick High School in Newport News. A member of the Isle of Wight Writers' Group and the Virginia Writers Club, she is listed in *Writers in Virginia*. Her poetry and fiction have been published in various journals, including Vols. 2, 3, and 4 of *The Poet's Domain*.

Leslie Sands

So who wants to buy this house?
The agent says it will be difficult
to sell in this market.
It's far too small.
Not nearly enough there.

Sandra Ginn Scoville

Flying

Vermillion and copper hues ignite
Pale rays of Indian summer.
Swirling leaves
Rise warm,
Fall chilled,
And I stand bare
Under empty branches.
Up the trunk I climb
Past the wren house,
Higher and higher.
In the topmost limb
I pause by a nest
Abandoned by catbirds.
Slowly I turn my head into the wind.
I simply need to stretch out my arms.
Autumn is the time for flight.

Sandra Ginn Scoville (b. 1939, Snow Hill, NC) was a member of poetry groups in New York and Belgium. She returned to the South in 1985 and is currently living, working, and writing on the Eastern Shore of Virginia. She has won a poetry award from the Writer's Circle in Charlotte, NC.

Lynda Self

Sequel

Some things secure, made fossil by the mind.
Others drift—lose their place somewhat and
    lodge anew,
distortion now mistook for fact.
Such as the cream you stirred into my coffee.

The room too changed—furniture
    repositioned,
altering now the angle of our view,
forcing us to greet on other terms. More
    careful
not to touch, we feel the rigor of such
    postures.

As if rather than revisiting each other,
we revisited ourselves, slightly skewed,
    unfocused,
like an image in an album—and nearly
    without lag,
the talk resumes, inhabited by the same or
    similar volumes.

And after parting, it weaves its tinsel through
    our minds.
Whatever substance had been lost regains a
    definition.
As if we thought that somehow we'd
    refurbish the rooms
we once moved through—and still not live
    there.

Lynda Self (b. 1943, Washington, DC) is chair of the English Department at Maury High School in Norfolk, VA. Her work appeared previously in Vol. 2 of *The Poet's Domain*.

Shirley Nesbit Sellers

The Castle

I began with just a pile of sand
And bits of driftwood found at hand,
But quite soon walls and towers took form
With drawbridged moat no foe could storm.

For hours the sun and I kept pace
to fill with fairy-lore that place,
Until its rays fell soft and late
Upon the moat and castle gate.

My back was to the rising tide
Where ancient green-eyed dragons ride.
One rode a wave from the ocean floor
And my feudal kingdom was no more.

Old Bay Line Steamer

The trip to Baltimore upon the bay
Was made throughout the night. The eager
    guest
Boarded when the sun was in the west
And harbor lights announced the end of day.
The sumptuous dining hall, at his behest,
Served by white-frocked men a grand cuisine;
Then, replete, he strolled outside to browse
    and lean
Against the rail—leaving the traveler's fest
To watch the steamer's lights upon dark green
Of prow-parted water, and the elegance of
    white
Hotel above him gliding through the night.
With grace and style, passing the shores
    between,
It plowed its rhythmic path through liquid
    loam,
A floating fairyland of light and foam.

Shirley Nesbit Sellers (b. 1926, Norfolk, VA), retired teacher, now storyteller and writer of children's stories, is resident of Norfolk, VA. She is currently vice-president of the Poetry Society of Virginia where she has received a number of awards for her "Norfolk poems."

Harry B. Sheftel

Bright Burning

Validated for a term of residence
on the Isle of Delos,
I received a dowry of twelve
bright candles upon my
signature of agreement. Each
candle was certified for a year
of life, each attuned to the length
of all the seasons...
                    I lit the first
on my birthdate, a ceremony akin to
a celebration of spring's vibrancy,
accepted it as a rare dispensation
granted to a human.
Its light prevailed all that year.
Then I lit the second. Its light
graced the months of that
year. On each successive birthday
I lit another to gain that most
precious gift. When the twelfth
was due, Island Custodians had no
need to remind me of the Prophecy.
I returned to my private cosmos after
lighting the twelfth
                    so that the Prophecy
might hold, that there be
                    no deaths on Delos.

Harry B. Sheftel (b. 1906, Clinton, MA), retired as economist, Office of Management & Budget, has published over 400 poems and 3 collections: *Quotations from my Questing, Of Truths and Wonderments,* and *From Alpha to Omega.* He is a member of Federal Poets and the Academy of American Poets. He lives in Washington, DC.

Askold Skalsky

Metaphysic's End

The man who defined space
As an ordered totality
Of concrete extensions
And spoke of the antithetical law
Of limitation and transcendence
Is gone now.

Praised as a paladin
Of rigorous intellectual inquiry
And the author of seminal texts,
He died at seventy-nine
In a small town in Canada
Known for its potash works.

Askold Skalsky (b. 1940, Ukraine) lives in Ijamsville, MD, and teaches at Hagerstown Junior College.

Barbara Smith

Lady Liberty Weekend
New York Harbor

Lady in reconditioned splendor
Was in scaffolding:
Her imprisonment reflects
Closed door feeling
Of Americans towards immigration

Tall ships fully unfurled
Libertad from Argentina
Esmeralda, controversial
Spectre of tortured
Political prisoners aboard.
Columbia's proud sailors
Welcomed visitors onto teak decks.

Inside ship South American music blared
Posters showing population
Products, lifestyles.
Young sailors spouting Spanish.
Harbor jammed—sailing vessels,
Warships, small craft, tall ships.

Lady sparkled, torch bright,
Standing tall, welcoming all.
Blacks came into harbor in chains,
Had no feeling towards Lady.

Barbara Smith (b. 1936, Newport News, VA) writes poetry, non-fiction, and fiction. She has published in *Orphic Lute, Currents, Great American Poetry Anthology, Cube Literary Magazine, Flights of Fancy*, and *Fictitious and True*. She won a poetry award at Christopher Newport College Writers' Conference. A member of Virginia Writers' Club, VCCA Writers in Virginia and Tidewater Writers' Association, she is a docent at the Mariner's Museum and works on a crisis telephone hotline. She visited and shot video in Tibet, Inner Mongolia, and other parts of China in 1991. She resides in Newport News, VA.

William Reuben Smith

Viewing the Great Nebula in the Dagger of Orion

It is cold—a good January night
for viewing the universe around us.
Seen through the scope, in Virginia's
clear and winter sky—there they are
four young, hot, blazing, blue suns
fresh from the incubator,
still in the glowing, gleaming nursery
of nebula. Beautiful, or were
those thousands of years ago
when the light we see left them.
Beauty, though, is not here reality.
Suns do not form without the violence
of ever-building gravity,
nor planets attach themselves
without fierce clashings and collisions.
Black holes may form, devouring all
within their reach.
From this elemental push and pull
have come the heavy atoms we must have
to be the humans that we are.
I look deep in your eyes and see that glint
And am startled and surprised.

William Reuben Smith (b. 1923, Carlisle, KY), a retired graduate of the U.S. Naval Academy, saw active duty in the World War II and Korean War periods. His 30-year engineering career included sailing as the first Nuclear Advisor aboard N.S. Savannah, a nuclear-powered merchantman. He is President and Newsletter Editor for *The Piedmont Literary Review*, a member of the Poetry Society of Virginia, and is listed in *Writers in Virginia*. His work has appeared in *The Piedmont Literary Review*, a Poetry Society of Virginia *Anthology of Poems by Member Poets*, Vol. 3 of *The Poet's Domain* series, and elsewhere. He lives in Lynchburg, VA.

William Reuben Smith

Maturity

Despite the aches, I'm thankful I can smile.
I find I need my glasses now to read.
My back is hurting—I must rest a while.
I still have hair to part, though thin's my style
confederate gray, and threatening to secede.
Despite the aches, I'm thankful I can smile.
My muscles tell me I'm no juvenile.
After weeding beds or stooping planting seed
my back is hurting—I must rest a while.
My teeth are sturdy—strong as crocodile—
so full of fillings cavities can't breed.
Despite the aches, I'm thankful I can smile.
Some nights leg muscles cramp as stiff as tile
and drive me from my bed—so fast indeed
my back is hurting—I must rest a while.
But living still is sweet. I'll not revile
a life there's much to smile about. My creed?
Despite the aches I'm thankful I can smile.
My back is hurting—I must rest a while.

Bruce Souders

Bruce Souders (b. 1920, Richland, PA) lives in Winchester, VA, where he is Professor Emeritus at Shenandoah University. A past president of the Poetry Society of Virginia, he has been published in *The Poet's Domain*, Vols. 3, 4, 5, and 6. He is currently writing the history of Shenandoah University and recently edited and published a collection of poetry by S. Gordden Link.

Ruminations in a Parking Lot

"That's not my car," I say
looking for license plates
now relegated to a landfill
for future anthropologists
to ponder. I try to suppress
change in any form.
I don't want to admit
I'm passing into history
little more than a footnote.

Like the Emperor of Ice-Cream,
I look for flowers wrapped
in "last month's newspapers."
My bouquet is one new
powder blue Corsica
that carried me across
potholed concrete lanes
of superhighway in four
contiguous states.

Apologia: A Collage of Remembrance

You'll find few images of hunting
in my poems. I have never
hunted or been hunted. In fact
my not hunting distressed
my grandfather, whose rifles and trophies
adorned his smoke-filled sanctuary
where he devoured Zane Grey repeatedly
and kept nightly council with Rosie,
his dog, and Polly the parrot.

But I made it up to him
when we wet our lines and skewered
our catch on the placid shores
of a nearby stream
and later still, when I—

Bruce Souders

his "grandson the tuba player"—
joined the old town band
where Grandpa played first chair
trombone for thirty years.

And as for being hunted,
Grandpa knew that only
criminals and animals are hunted.
Criminals grew up in cities,
not sleepy little hamlets.
Then, too, our kin had earned
security against invasion
by fighting the Great War
that saved the world for Democracy.

Isobel Routly Stewart

The Dark Clouds Part

You could not dare the wound of openness,
the giving of yourself we know as love.
"You needn't be afraid I'll ever leave you.
You love me more, much more, than I love
 you,
but where else could I go?"
You told me once,
"It was a disappointment
on our wedding night
to find your breasts so large."
How could you have known
my guilty shyness grew
at least in portion from that fact?
Let us be friends again
as once we were,
before we married fifty years ago.
Too long I've brooded on unkindly words
startling as thunder on my brightest days.

Ten years ago you put aside the flesh
that ached and prisoned you.
Lately I have understood your sorrow:
your weaknesses
had made me strong for you,
your illness,
growing,
forced me into health;
but reaching joy became a threat to you
though it was fostered only for your sake.
You had no option
but to tear me down,
to comrade you in your unhappiness—
and it is I who needs to be forgiven.

Rest easy now.
At last, I haven you
among my happiest memories.

Isobel Routly Stewart (b. 1917, Toronto, Canada) is published regularly in a number of little magazines and annually self-publishes her year's work for interested friends—*Life is for Dreaming, Loving Life, Shadow of the Middle East,* and *Island Healing* are recent titles. Her work has appeared in *The Poet's Domain*, Vols. 2 through 6.

Isobel Routly Stewart

Appointment with the Vet

No longer can you share the morning run,
your failing hips create a swivel walk
until your legs give way
and tumble you.
You never whimper
but your mouth is drawn,
the tail is quiet,
eyes pursue us as we move about.

When they lay you on the table,
I'll hold your head between my hands
and smile at you.
You'll hardly feel
the flea bite of the final needle.

You'll drift to sleep.
I hope you'll dream—
happy dreams about your Blue Ridge romps,
your guardianship of our front porch
with fierce stentorian barks;
may they fade to quieter dreams
of sleeping in the sun,
of rubbing noses with your favorite cat.

I know that you are ready, long have been.
I am the one who could not say goodbye.

Kathryn A. Strickland

Hour Glass

Hold your breath and count to three,
and join me in my reverie:

Exhale the sand
filtering through your system.
Accompany me to my desert.

The Arab drags his tattered sandals
across broken cracks in the pavement.
His prayer call can wait.

Drip! Drip! Drop!
from the ancient radiator
clinging to a damp wall.

Horns blare from automobiles
screeching in disgust
at an extinct generation.
Never mind lending a hand
to the tired female
wearing her black costume everyday.

Flip the hour glass.
See, the same
will happen
all over
again.

Kathryn A. Strickland (b. 1972, San Diego, CA) is double-majoring in English and Communication Studies at Virginia Tech. She resides in Blacksburg and frequently visits her parents, who have been working in Dhahran, Saudi Arabia, for eight years.

Hilda (Boyce) Sweikhart

A Humility of Valor

You walked so slipper-soft upon the earth
your feet scarce stirred the restless sands of
    time
and though your name now unembellished
    lies
midst tales of family heroes from another time
you had valor of a different kind.

You laughed and loved as though you didn't
    know
your useless legs had such a little way to go
and sang sweet-forever songs of timeless love
to comfort her.
As though you didn't know
that soon she'd carve in stone above your
    head

"My Ebenezer died...age 35...He was a
    peaceable man."

The Lamb's Cry

I found you, orphaned Lamb,
huddled against a rock,
in only-imagined security.

I kept you warm for a season,
then wept in another spring

to find you too early shorn,
shivering and cold, in an
icy mountain ravine.

Hilda (Boyce) Sweikhart (b. 1914, Fairmont, WV), won an Honorable Mention in Baltimore City poetry awards. A collection of her poetry and a novella are almost complete. She lives in Baltimore.

D. Lynn Sydow

Complements

I am sun-beaten sand,
wind-creviced fields,
hermetically-sealed cotton,
dehydrated pear,
August noon's pavement.

You are evening tide,
life-lending rain,
fresh azalea bloom,
prime ripe melon,
cool spring cumulonimbus

I am antechamber,
prelude, forward, preface,
ruptured amnion,
flash of life,
thumb-readied hammer

You are grand ballroom
acts 1-5, epic poem, classic novel,
vermillion placenta,
jaunt to Byzantium
bull's eye.

I am Appalachian woman
ancient mountain soul
bare feet, bare body, bare mind
swallow in flight
modern day Spinoza

You are midwestern man
street wise survivor
would-be cowboy
prey-driven hawk
practitioner of Hobbes

"And the Lord God formed man
of the dust of the ground, and breathed
into his nostrils the breath of life;
and man became a living soul.

D. Lynn Sydow
(b. 1961, Norton, VA) teaches composition and literature at Southwest Virginia Community College in Richlands, VA. She is an active member of the Appalachian Center for Poets and Writers and resides in Lebanon, VA.

D. Lynn Sydow

And the Lord God said, It is not good
that the man should be alone...and from
the
rib, which the Lord God had taken from
man,
made he a woman, and brought her unto
the man.

And they were both naked,
the man and his wife,
and were not ashamed."

Constance Tupper

Dear Friend

Dear friend,
I remember you in whilom days,
Youth, dancing us wildly on his knee;
Kicking to his varied tunes,
You rode your cock-horse
Down ways I never dared to run.

War was a hurricane
Spinning you clockwise,
New York to London blitz,
While I, cushioned in the eye,
Shrank from the roil,
Feeling a twang of envy.

Now after years of silence,
I do not want to know if you are dead.

Constance Tupper (b. 1919, Manhattan, NY) is an artist who has lived in Virginia for over 30 years. A member of the Poetry Society of Virginia, she has had poems published in *The Poet's Domain*, Vols. 2 through 6, and in *Orphic Lute*. In 1976 she won a Merit Award from *Woman's Day* magazine for her essay "Women, Today and Tomorrow." In 1992 she won an Honorable Mention in the Poetry Society of Virginia's annual contest.

Gonny Van den Broek

For Him Who Thinks He Sinned

Oh no, do not confess, it won't make sense
To whisper it to preachers of a church!
A sin? A law? How gross a violation
To eye a winking light along your way?
To cling to the glare of its attraction
Like wildlife in the high beams of a car;
Transfixed to hold, to love a while, to waver,
Before reversing—each his chosen path?

I wouldn't even share it with a friend
For fear that if defensively detoured
You may no longer race throughout my being
But take the sharpest turning—inward out—
And crash within a traffic-jam of words.

Though if you fear and must, go to your
    church
Not for the penance of a law unyielding
But for a prayer to the Judge above.
And yes, add one on my behalf to thank Him
For that which will outlive our dead-end love.

Before Boarding

This time it's fragrance—
cologne, that romantic brand,
the kind, it seemed,
patented for you alone;
now wafting from a stranger
here at the airport.
Ah, I inhale again
all of you,
all of us,
immerse in memories,
see splashes of tearful attempts
to hold on.

Gonny Van den Broek (b. 1939, Netherlands) has just taken early retirement from her job as Administrative Assistant at an international organization to devote more time to writing. Her poetry has been published in the *New York Times*, *The Christian Science Monitor*, *The Lyric*, *The Federal Poet* and in numerous other poetry publications. She has also won several prizes in poetry contests.

Gonny Van den Broek

I remember your saying,
"Later, looking back,
you'll laugh it off."

Over the years
I've often looked back,
often turned around
for your voice, gestures,
or such stinging aftershaves.

Say, where did I laugh?

Evelyn Amuedo Wade

Lists

At night when I can't sleep, I make lists.
Lists of people I should write to,
names of towns I passed as I drove
through Pennsylvania, the exact titles
of all the courses I took in college.

I make lists of words like
fiddle faddle,
helter skelter,
shilly shally,
and hodge podge.

I make lists of the good and the bad
in my character—a kind of moral inventory—
and because I have a redeeming need
to be honest with myself
the bad always outweighs the good.

I make lists of the teachers I had
in grammar school who taught me about
Marco Polo, how to do long division,
and what the chief exports are in Peru,
but who failed to teach me that
the heart, closeted away beneath
a prison cell of ribs,
is just as vulnerable grown up
as it was in the fourth grade.

And I wonder why "grown-up"
didn't turn out to be all the freedom
and the laughter and flirtation,
all the do-as-I-want-to-do
they told me it would be
when I was nine.

Evelyn Amuedo Wade (b. New Orleans, LA) holds degrees from American and George Washington Universities. She has lived in Virginia for forty-seven years and has published hundreds of pieces in dozens of publications in this country and in Great Britain and taken many national awards for her poetry and her fiction. Professor Emeritus in the Virginia Community College System, she has two published books of poetry and two children's books.

Temple West

Mother Myth

Persephone's mythical journey
like mine—through death's door.
She is a maiden.
I am only seven.
Hades is her abductor.
My father abducted me.
Demeter, the mother who
rants and raves and strikes
the world barren
searching for her daughter.

"Mother, did you look for me?"

Temple West (b. 1947, Hanover, NH), a massage therapist in Norfolk, VA, is publishing her poetry for the first time in this edition. She is currently working on a series of poems based on her massage experience.

Charlotte Wise

The Market of Words

Townsfolk of Tok know the Yokomore tree,
which stands guard for the market of words;
they know the tangle of yarrow that grows
and the yawp...yawp of tropical birds.

There in the yarrow they barter their wares
for the yardage of wordage they need;
trading their worn-out expressions for new
costs them often a sentence indeed!

"Tokmen, your muscle and brawn may be
 bought—
right this way," shouts a boy in the street.
There they replenish their masculine words:
acrobatic, aquatic, athlete.

Cupid is always a word in demand,
also *moonlight, caress* and *amour:*
Music, romance and large orders of *love*
bring a price from the ardent Tokwooer.

Nights may be long, but Tokfolk are prepared
with somniferous *slumber* and *rest;*
they seek for sandman's drowsy *repose*
and *snoozle* on Morpheus' breast.

If you should follow the yarrow that grows
and give ear to the yawp...yawp of birds,
you would discover the Yokomore tree
and go into the Market of Words.

Charlotte Wise (b. , Richmond, VA) attended William & Mary and Columbia University. She participated in the Breadloaf Writer's Conference and a literary seminar at Cambridge University. Her poetry and fiction appeared in *Southern Literary Messenger, Saturday Review of Literature, Bozart-Westminster* (England), *The Stepladder*, anthologies and chapbooks. She lives in Wintergreen, VA, and New Orleans, writes free-lance, and reviews books. She is active in the Poetry Society of Virginia.

Moraeg E. Wood

Flotsam and Jetsam

As the sea surges
To the shore
Then leaves again
So do the generations
Come, then go.

On sandy beaches
And in rocky places
The sea casts
Its hoarded bits
And leaves them there.

It is the same with us.
We leave small fragments
Of ourselves, our time,
For some future seeker
To cast aside or even
Venerate as treasure.

Moraeg E. Wood (b. 1914, Jamaica, NY) moved to Charlottesville, VA, in 1986. She is a Foster Grandmother for two first-grade classes, where she, of course, promotes poetry. She won the Grand Prize in the Crossroads Contest in 1981 and has had poems published in a number of publications, including *The Connecticut River Review* and *Turtle Magazine*.

Israel Zoberman

Years Later

Somehow I omit your name
from the guest list
though you may not know.
And years later
I still feel the sting.

Places & Lovers

Ever attempting to recall
places I've been to
to preserve their enchantment,
I remember a past beloved,
not wishing to forget.

Israel Zoberman (b. 1945, Chu, Kazakhastan, USSR), ordained as a reform rabbi by the Hebrew Union College—Jewish Institute of Religion in 1974, has been rabbi to Congregation Beth Chaverim in Virginia Beach since 1985. He studied at the University of Illinois and McCormick Theological Seminary (the only rabbi to receive a Doctor of Ministry in Pastoral Care and Counseling from this Presbyterian institution). His poetry and his translations from Hebrew have been published in *CCAR Journal*, the *Jewish Spectator*, the *American Rabbi, Moment*, and *The Poet's Domain*, Vols. 5 and 6.